Advanced Nunchaku

Advanced Nunchaku

by
Fumio Demura and Dan Ivan

Edited by Geri Adachi

© 1976 Ohara Publications, Incorporated
All rights reserved
Printed in the United States of America
Library of Congress Catalog Card Number: 76-40816
ISBN 0-89750-021-0

Graphic Design/Nancy Hom Lem
Photography/Ed Ikuta

Thirth-fifth printing 2002

WARNING

OHARA ⦿ PUBLICATIONS, INCORPORATED
SANTA CLARITA, CALIFORNIA

dedication

To the late Okinawan karate master, Kenshin Taira, that perfect example of the gentle spirit of the martial arts, who was initially responsible for our interest and subsequent skill in kobu-do; to Yasutsune Itosu and Kenwa Mabuni, revered masters who are the grandfathers of modern kobu-do and karate; and to Ryusho Sakagami, honored instructor.

acknowledgements

To our three very dedicated young disciples: Chuck Lanza, Steve Ambuter and Makoto Ibushi who posed for the photographs.

about the authors

Fumio Demura, 5th-dan, was born in Yokohama, Japan. He began his martial arts training with kendo and later studied aikido and judo. While at Nihon University in Tokyo, he earned a bachelor of science degree in economics and, at the same time, developed a keen interest in kobu-do (the use of weapons such as the bo, the sai, the tonfa, the kama and the nunchaku) which he studied under the tutelage of Kenshin Taira and Ryusho Sakagami.

Noted in Japan as an outstanding karateka, Demura won the All-Japan Karate Free-Style Tournament in 1961 and, for the three consecutive years from 1961 to 1964, he was among Japan's top eight players. His numerous tournament wins include the East Japan, the Shito-Ryu Annual and the Kanto District championships. Demura has also received the All-Japan Karate Federation President's trophy for outstanding tournament play and has been awarded certificates of recognition from Japanese Cabinet officials for his achievements in and contributions to the art of karate. He now directs the U.S. division of the Japan Karate Federation and serves as an advisor to the Pan-American Karate Association.

In 1969, BLACK BELT Magazine's Hall of Fame honored Demura's dedication to karate by naming him Karate Sensei of the Year. In 1974, he received martial arts' Golden Fist award and, in 1975, was again honored by the BLACK BELT Hall of Fame, this time as their Martial Artist of the Year.

Demura's first book, *SHITO-RYU KARATE*, was published in 1971. His three later books, *NUNCHAKU, Karate Weapon of Self-Defense; SAI, Karate Weapon of Self-Defense* and *BO, Karate Weapon of Self-Defense*, each introduce a weapon of kobu-do.

Fumio Demura   Dan Ivan

Dan Ivan has been an active practitioner of the martial arts for over 30 years. One of the first Americans to earn a black belt in aikido, he also holds black belts in karate, kendo and judo. Ivan opened his first dojo in 1956 and was one of the first sensei contracted to teach self-defense techniques to local law enforcement personnel.

Ivan also spent 13 years with the U.S. Army. During these years, his extensive work with intelligence, military police and provost marshall units included numerous assignments in the Orient, as a C.I.D. investigator. Working undercover, Ivan often found that his martial arts expertise and his fluency in Japanese were essential to his survival. His experiences as a military criminal investigator are profiled in his first book, *TOKYO UNDERCOVER*, and have provided him with material for articles in leading adventure magazines. Ivan also writes a regular self-defense column for KARATE ILLUSTRATED magazine.

In 1971, Ivan was named director of the first team representing the United States in the World Championships in Tokyo. In 1972, BLACK BELT Magazine's Hall of Fame chose him as their Man of the Year.

The Demura-Ivan association began in 1965 when Ivan invited Demura to teach Shito-Ryu karate in the United States. Together, they now own and operate a string of dojo in southern California.

authors' preface

True martial artists, always considered men of honor and dignity, hold great reverence for their kobu-do weapons. They consider the nunchaku an asset in further developing their overall dexterity and coordination. Recently, however, the nunchaku has become not only one of the most popular but one of the most controversial of the kobu-do weapons.

Because of its simple construction—two sticks joined together by a length of rope or chain—the nunchaku is relatively inexpensive to purchase or to make oneself. Recently, though, it has fallen into public disfavor. In some states, legislation prohibits possession or use of the weapon. We are of the opinion that although the nunchaku has been faddishly popularized in a rash of martial arts movies, only a handful of the disreputable element has misused it.

The fact that the common kitchen knife takes part more often in accidents and crimes of violence, with less adverse publicity, is proof in itself that the nunchaku has been unjustly criticized. What we are trying to point out is that responsibility lies not in the nature of the weapon but in the nature of its users. Seldom, if ever, has it been reported to us that an accomplished karateka has used the nunchaku improperly. For this reason, we appeal to all dedicated martial artists to help police our "own."

Let us work together to do everything legally within our means to see that only trusted members of our martial arts community practice the nunchaku.

Fumio Demura
Dan Ivan
Orange County, California
1976

contents

methods of grasping the nunchaku | 13

swinging and striking techniques | 17

changing grasps | 49

double flips | 57

combinations | 79

double nunchaku | 91

ideas for self·defense | 105

kata | 131

methods of grasping the nunchaku

To learn the advanced nunchaku techniques which are included in this text, first become very familiar with these ways of grasping the weapons. These holds and grasps are meant to supplement the basic grasps learned in *NUNCHAKU, Karate Weapon of Self-Defense* by Fumio Demura, Ohara Publications, Inc., 1971. The applications shown along with these advanced grasps exemplify only a few of the possibilities. Through practice, you can devise countless others.

GRASP ON BOTTOM END

GRASP IN MIDDLE

GRASP AT TOP END

REVERSE GRASP IN MIDDLE

REVERSE GRASP ON TOP END
(BOTTOM POINTS UPWARD)

swinging and striking techniques

Swinging strikes, sometimes described as whipping, are the very essence of nunchaku techniques. While you may, on occasion, use the nunchaku to jab, thrust or block, it serves you best in swinging movements.

The recovery after your swing is most important. If you swing your weapon with full force and cannot recover it skillfully, you may hit or injure yourself. Safe recovery may be completed by simply expending the swing, recoiling the weapon off or wrapping it around part of your body, or catching it from a different angle.

This section deals with swinging the nunchaku and recovering it safely. It also shows you how to maneuver your weapon from one hand to the other and how to change your type of grasp. While some of the techniques (the foot return, for instance) may seem of little functional value in and of themselves, they are important because they provide you with a means of catching or recovering your weapon. Again, keep in mind that your swing is intended both to strike an opponent and return to you *SAFELY*.

As you practice not only these techniques but those throughout the book, swing your weapon as though actually hitting a real opponent. This will help give force to your movements and will make clearer the purpose of each action.

VERTICAL SWING

(1) Assume a kamae (ready) position. Use your right hand to grasp one handle and let the other handle hang down behind your right shoulder. (2-3) Attack by slipping the nunchaku forward and down. (4) As your weapon completes its movement, unfurl the fingers of your right hand. (5) Recover by allowing the nunchaku handles to hit against each other. Then, close your right hand over both handles.

SIDE RETURN
(1) With your right hand, hold one handle firmly over your right shoulder. With your left hand, hold the other handle loosely behind you. (2-3) Release your left hand and strike out to your left diagonally. (4-5) Allow the loose handle to hit against and recoil off your left side. Now, for the return, in a continuous motion, reverse directions and swing the nunchaku forward. (6) Hold your left hand ready and, (7-8) as the free handle swings back to your right, grasp it firmly.

2

3

5

6

8

**SIDE RETURN
APPLICATION**

INNER THIGH RETURN

(1) Assume a wide stance. With your right hand, hold one handle firmly over your right shoulder. With your left, hold the other handle loosely behind you. (2-3) Release your left hand and strike downward. (4-5) Allow the loose handle to hit against and bounce off your inner right thigh. Then, in a continuous motion, reverse directions and swing the nunchaku forward and up. (6) Hold your left hand ready and, (7) as the free handle swings upward, grasp it firmly.

**INNER THIGH RETURN
APPLICATION**

SHOULDER RETURN

(1) Assume a wide stance. With your right hand, hold one handle firmly over your right shoulder. With your left, hold the other handle loosely behind you. (2-4) Release your left hand and strike downward, allowing the loose handle to hit against and bounce off your inner right thigh. (5-6) Smoothly swing the nunchaku upward and recoil it off your left shoulder. (7-8) Strike downward and allow the free handle again to hit against and bounce off your inner right thigh. (9-10) Swing the nunchaku upward and (11) return the loose handle to its original position behind you.

This set of movements may be repeated recoiling the nunchaku off *either* shoulder.

NECK CATCH
(1) Use your right hand to grasp one handle and let the other handle hang down behind your right shoulder. (2-4) Swing the nunchaku out and around horizontally. (5) As it sweeps to your extreme

left, reach back deeply with your right arm, wrapping the nunchaku around the back of your neck. (6) Cross your left hand over your right arm and grasp the loose handle.

NECK RETURN

(1) Use your right hand to grasp one handle and let the other handle hang down behind your right shoulder. (2-4) Swing the nunchaku out and around horizontally. (5) As it sweeps to your left, allow the weapon to wrap itself around, then recoil off the back of your neck. (6-8) Now, reverse directions, striking as you return the nunchaku to its original position.

UPWARD CATCH

(1) Use your right hand to grasp one handle and let the other handle hang down behind your right shoulder. Hold your open left hand extended high before you. (2-4) Sharply swing the nunchaku forward, downward and back on your right side. (5-6) Now, using a sharp wrist movement, snap the weapon forward. (7) As the loose handle swings upward, catch it with your left hand.

ARM RETURN

(1) Use your right hand to grasp one handle and let the other handle hang down behind your right upper arm. Hold your left arm extended on your left side at stomach level. (2-3) Swing the nunchaku out and around horizontally, (4) allowing the loose handle to hit against and recoil off your left upper arm. (5-7) Reverse directions and bring the weapon back to its original position behind your upper right arm.

This technique may be repeated, alternately catching the nunchaku first on one upper arm, then the other.

KNEE RETURN

(1) Assume a right zenkutsu-dachi (forward stance). With your right hand, hold one handle firmly over your right shoulder. With your left hand, hold the other handle loosely behind you. (2-3) Release your left hand and swing the nunchaku inward and down, (4) allowing the free handle to hit against and bounce off the back of your right knee. (5-6) Reverse directions and (7) bring the nunchaku back to its original position over your right shoulder.

You may repeat this technique, alternately bouncing the loose handle off your knee, then your shoulder.

1

FOOT RETURN

(1) Use your right hand to grasp one handle and let the other handle hang down behind your right shoulder. (2) Sweep the nunchaku outward and down. As you do so, raise your left foot for the recovery, (3) allowing the loose handle to bounce off your left sole. (4-5) Reverse directions and (6) return to your original position.

4

REVERSE GRASP/
SIDE RETURN

(1) With your right hand, use the reverse grasp to hold one handle, the bottom end pointing upward, out on your right side. Use your left hand in the normal grasp to hold the other handle in a horizontal

position. (2-4) Release the hold of your left hand and swing the weapon forward, out and around horizontally. (5) Allow the free handle to hit against and bounce off your left side just beneath your armpit.

UNDERARM GRASPING

(1) With your right hand, hold one handle loosely over your right shoulder. With your left hand, hold the other handle firmly behind you. (2-4) Release your right hand and whip the nunchaku forward and up to strike. (5-6) Continue the swing and bring the weapon up, around and behind your left shoulder. (7) Slip your right hand beneath your left arm and firmly catch the free handle. (8-11) Release your left hand. Now, use your right to swing the weapon in the opposite direction, moving it out, around and over your right shoulder. (12) Slip your left hand beneath your right arm and firmly catch the free handle to return to your original position.

Repeat this technique to develop speed and coordination.

BACK GRAB

(1) With your right hand, use the reverse grasp to hold one handle before you, the bottom end angled upward. With your left hand, hold the other handle normally near your left side. (2) Release your left hand and strike forward. (3-4) Now, sweep the weapon out, around and down behind you diagonally. As you do so, rotate your right hand counterclockwise 180 degrees. Begin reaching back with your left hand. (5) As your right hand moves behind your lower back, use your left hand, palm toward the ceiling, to catch the free handle with the normal grasp. (6-7) Release your right hand. Swing the nunchaku forward, out and up diagonally, rotating your left hand counterclockwise 180 degrees as you do so. (8) Now, smoothly bring the weapon high up over your left shoulder in readiness for a strike with your left hand.

46

47

changing grasps

Learning to move your nunchaku from one hand to the other, one grasp to another, is important. However, it is equally essential that you know how to change grasps using only one hand. In situations where only one of your hands is free, this skill will enable you to switch grasps and prepare yourself effectively for different types of strikes.

TWIRLING

(1) With your right hand extended before you, palm facing downward, hold one handle angled toward the floor. Let the other handle hang free. (2-6) Rotate the nunchaku clockwise, (7) allowing the loose handle to move over, around and under your right wrist. (8) As the weapon moves into a 360-degree turn, detach your right hand. (9-10) Then, as the nunchaku continues its spin, swiftly and firmly use your right hand in the reverse grasp to catch what was initially the free handle.

Execution of this technique requires manipulating the nunchaku in a continuous, smooth circular motion.

TWIRLING APPLICATION

REVERSE TWIRLING

(1) With your right hand extended before you in the reverse grasp, palm toward the ceiling, hold one handle parallel to the floor. Let the other handle hang free. (2-4) Rotate the nunchaku counterclockwise, allowing the loose handle to move outside, around and over your right wrist. (5) As the weapon moves into a 360-degree turn, detach your right hand. (6-7) Then, as the nunchaku continues its spin, swiftly and firmly use your right hand in the normal grasp to catch what was initially the free handle.

As with the twirling technique, execution of reverse twirling requires moving the nunchaku in a continuous circular motion.

54

double flips

Double flipping, swinging the nunchaku in multiple movements such as two circles or "figure eights," functions in several ways. You may use it to frighten your opponent with its flashing action or you may use it to generate more speed and velocity before a strike. In executing an attack, you may use both flips to hit your target or you may shorten the first flip to test your range, then, on the second movement, strike to hit the target.

DOUBLE OVERHEAD CIRCLES

(1) Grasping toward the bottom end of each handle, use both hands to hold the nunchaku above you horizontally. (2-4) Release your left hand and swing the nunchaku overhead in a clockwise circle, striking as the weapon moves forward. (5-6) Then, smoothly move into a second clockwise circle, again striking as the weapon comes forward. (7-8) As the nunchaku approaches completion of the second 360-degree sweep, reach up with your left hand and catch the free handle to return to your original position.

Double overhead circles may also be executed in a counterclockwise direction using your left hand to swing the nunchaku instead of your right.

**DOUBLE OVERHEAD
CIRCLES APPLICATION**

DOUBLE SIDE CIRCLES

(1) With your right hand, hold one handle firmly over your right shoulder. With your left hand, position the other handle behind your right arm and hold it against your right side. (2-5) Release your left hand and strike forward, down and around, completing a wide 360-degree counterclockwise sweep on your right side. (6-7) Smoothly begin a second sweep, bringing the nunchaku down to a hanging position near your right leg. Pause. (8-10) Then, reverse directions and swing the weapon over and behind your right shoulder. Slip your left hand beneath your right arm, catching the free handle to return to your original position.

Double side circles may also be executed using counterclockwise and clockwise circles instead of two counterclockwise circles.

ONE HAND FLIPPING

(1) With your right hand, hold the nunchaku before you, handles together and parallel to the floor. (2-4) Releasing one of the handles, swing it downward, out, upward and back to complete, on a plane perpendicular to your body, a small circle before you. (5) Smoothly begin a second circle. (6) Then, as the free handle approaches completion of its second rotation, unfurl your right hand and catch it firmly.

Practice this technique using your left hand as well as your right.

FLIPPING, CHANGING HANDS

(1) Use both hands, a handle in each, to hold the nunchaku before you. (2-5) Release your left hand and swing the loose handle downward, out, upward and back to complete, on a plane perpendicular to your body, a small circle in front of you. (6) Smoothly begin a second circle. (7) Then, as the free handle approaches completion of its second rotation, catch it firmly with your left hand.

You may also practice this set of movements using your left hand to swing the weapon and your right to catch and recover.

DOWNWARD SWING

(1) Grasping toward the bottom end of each handle, use both hands to hold the nunchaku above you horizontally. (2-5) Release your left hand but keep it poised above your head. Swing the nunchaku outward, down, forward and to the far left in a wide clockwise circle before you. (6-7) Then, smoothly move into a second wide clockwise circle. (8) As the loose handle completes the second 360-degree sweep, catch it firmly overhead with your left hand.

During the downward swing of the wide circular sweep, the loose handle may be aimed at lower targets such as an opponent's leg or shin.

REVERSE GRASP SWING

(1) With your right hand, use the reverse grasp to hold one handle out on your right side, the bottom end pointing upward. Use your left hand in the normal grasp to hold the other handle in a horizontal position. (2-5) Release your left hand and, on a plane roughly parallel to the floor, swing the weapon before you in a counterclockwise circle. (6-8) Smoothly move into a second counterclockwise circle. Hold your open left hand poised out on your left side. (9) As the free handle approaches completion of the second 360-degree swing, use your left hand to catch it firmly on your left side.

In addition to two counterclockwise circles, you may also use this general technique to complete two clockwise circles or two "figure eights."

70

**REVERSE GRASP SWING
APPLICATION**

INNER THIGH RETURN

(1) Use your right hand to grasp one handle and let the other handle hang down behind your right shoulder. Assume a wide stance. (2-4) Strike forward and down, allowing the loose handle to hit against and recoil off your inner right thigh. (5-7) On the return, smoothly swing the nunchaku into a clockwise circle before you. (8-9) On completing the rotation, recover by swinging the weapon up over your right shoulder and return to your original position.

This technique differs from the inner thigh return shown in *Striking and Swinging* in two ways: (1) while in the earlier sequence two hands are used to make the recovery, here only one hand is used throughout the technique; (2) rather than the single movement of the earlier technique, a flip here is also used just prior to recovery.

UNDERARM CATCH

(1) Clamp one handle tightly under your right armpit and hold the other handle firmly with your right hand. (2) Push your right elbow outward and swiftly snap the handle under your armpit forward. (3-7) Extend your right arm and trace a "figure eight" with the weapon, beginning the configuration on your right side. (8-9) As you complete the "figure eight," raise your right elbow and snap the free handle back to its original position under your right armpit.

combinations

This section deals with various combinations of grasps and strikes. Proficiency in using combinations best prepares you for surprise attacks. It enables you to respond fluidly from many different angles and positions.

Fast, smooth nunchaku combinations minimize the possibility of defeat and, in addition to the examples given here, it is recommended that you work on developing your own sets of combinations.

OVERHEAD CIRCLE/
NECK CATCH

(1) Grasping toward the bottom of each handle, use both hands to hold the nunchaku above you horizontally. (2-4) Release your left hand and swing the nunchaku overhead in a wide clockwise circle. (5) Begin a second clockwise sweep but, as the weapon approaches your extreme left, lower it to neck level. (6) Reach back deeply with your right arm, wrapping the nunchaku around the back of your neck. (7) To recover, cross your left hand over your right and grasp the free handle firmly.

INNER THIGH RETURN/
OPPOSITE HAND CATCH

(1) With your right hand, hold one handle firmly over your right shoulder. With your left, hold the other handle loosely behind you. Assume a wide stance. (2-3) Release your left hand and strike downward, allowing the loose handle to hit against and recoil off your inner right thigh. (4) Then, in a continuous motion, reverse directions and snap the nunchaku forward and up, (5-6) catching the free handle with your left hand. (7-8) Release your right hand and swing the weapon upward and back, (9) allowing the loose handle to hit against and bounce off your left shoulder. (10-11) Reverse directions and again strike downward smoothly, this time allowing the free handle to strike against and bounce off your inner left thigh. (12-13) Then, in a continuous motion, reverse directions and snap the nunchaku forward and up, (14-16) securely catching the free handle with your right hand.

SIDE RETURN/HAND CATCH, TECHNIQUE I

(1) With your right hand, hold one handle firmly over your right shoulder. With your left, hold the other handle loosely behind you. (2-4) Release your left hand and strike forward and down on your outside right. (5-6) Reverse directions and snap the weapon forward and up, allowing it to hit against and recoil off your right shoulder. (7-9) Now, smoothly swing the nunchaku forward to your left side, this time allowing it to hit against and bounce off the left side of your body. (10-12) On the return, snap the free handle up and to the right, catching it firmly with your left hand.

SIDE RETURN/HAND CATCH, TECHNIQUE II

(1) With your right hand, hold one handle firmly over your right shoulder. With your left, hold the other handle loosely behind you. (2-4) Release your left hand and whip the nunchaku out and around in a horizontal circle. (5-6) Begin a second, wider horizontal sweep. (7) As the weapon approaches your left side, lower it to solar plexus level and allow it to hit against and bounce off the left side of your body. (8-10) Reverse directions and snap the nunchaku forward and up, securely catching the free handle with your left hand.

ARM RETURN/SIDE CIRCLE

(1) With your right hand, hold one handle firmly over your right upper arm. With your left, hold the other handle loosely behind it. (2-4) Release your left hand and swing the nunchaku out and around horizontally, allowing the loose handle to hit against and bounce off your left upper arm. (5-7) Reverse directions and swing the weapon back to your right, this time allowing the free handle to hit against and recoil off your right upper arm. (8-10) Now, strike forward and down on your outside right. (11-12) Then, reverse directions again and swing the weapon up, over and behind your right upper arm. (13) Slip your left hand beneath your right arm, catching the free handle to return to your original position.

double nunchaku

The advantages of using two nunchaku are obvious. Fighting with two weapons instead of one doubles not only your striking power, but your capacity to hit and block as well. Of course, the obvious disadvantage of handling two weapons is the increased risk of hitting or injuring yourself. Using two nunchaku does require considerably more skill and practice on your part, but, because "double nunchaku" techniques are both impressive to watch and highly effective defensive maneuvers, proficiency in them is well worth the effort.

Initially, practice the "double nunchaku" techniques presented here using only one weapon, running through the movements first with one hand, then the other. Then, as you become more adept, use two weapons. Remember also that at first these techniques will be easier if you grasp the middle of the handles rather than the tops or bottoms.

VERTICAL SWING

(1) With your arms extended easily at your sides, hold a nunchaku, handles together, in each hand. (2-4) Unfurl your fingers, releasing one handle of each weapon, and swing upward and over, allowing the nunchaku to hit against and recoil off your shoulders. (5-7) Reverse directions and strike forward and down with a snap, allowing the handles of each weapon to hit against each other. To avoid hitting your fingers here, remember to pinch the handles securely between your thumbs and palms only. Keep your fingers extended and out of the way. Then, as the handles come together, close your hands over them.

SIDE RETURN
(1) Firmly grasp one handle of each weapon and hold them over your upper arms. Let the other handle of each hang down behind you. (2-4) Swing forward, crossing your arms before you, left over right. Allow the weapons to hit against and recoil off the sides of your body (the nunchaku in your right hand hitting the left side of your body; the nunchaku in your left hand hitting the right side of your body). (5-7) Then, reverse directions, bringing the weapons back to their original position.

2

4

5

7

"FIGURE EIGHT" SWING

(1) Firmly grasp one handle of each weapon and hold them over your shoulders. Let the other handle of each hang down behind you. (2-6) Moving them inward, down, upward and back, trace "figure eights" with the weapons. Cross and uncross your left arm over your right as you do so. (7) As you complete the configurations, hold the nunchaku poised in an upright position, handles in alignment. (8-9) Then, strike downward on your sides. (10-11) Reverse directions and swing the nunchaku back to their original position.

UNDERARM CATCH

(1) Clamp one handle of each weapon under an armpit. Firmly hold the other handle of each with your hands. (2-3) Push your elbows outward and swiftly snap the handles under your armpits forward and

3

down in a circular movement. (4) As they come backward and up, raise your elbows slightly and catch the free handles under your armpits to return to your original position.

4

REVERSE SIDE CIRCLE/
INNER THIGH RETURN

(1) Firmly grasp one handle of each weapon and hold them over your shoulders. Let the other handle of each hang down over your back. (2-4) Strike downward, allowing the nunchaku to hit against and recoil off your inner thighs. (5-7) Reversing directions, swing the nunchaku in circles at your sides. (8-9) As you complete a 360-degree rotation with each, swing the weapons upward to return them to their original position.

INNER THIGH RETURN/SHOULDER RETURN/UNDERARM CATCH

(1) Clamp one handle of each weapon under an armpit. Firmly hold the other handle of each with your hands. Assume a wide stance. (2-4) Push your elbows outward and swiftly snap the handles under your armpits forward and down, allowing them to hit against and recoil off your inner thighs. (5-7) Reverse directions and swing the nunchaku upward, allowing them to hit against and bounce off your shoulders. (8) On the return, swing the weapons forward and down in circular movements. (9-10) As the free handles come backward and up, raise your elbows slightly and catch the loose handles under your armpits to return to your original position.

102

ideas for self·defense

All nunchaku movements are designed for self-defense. This section, however, presents several specific methods you may wish to study and use. Again, with practice, you should be able to devise many of your own self-defense techniques. The potential combinations here are virtually limitless.

DEFENSE AGAINST GRABBING

(1) Hold the nunchaku, handles together, in your right hand and face your opponent. (2) As your opponent grabs your right wrist, (3-4) twist your hand so that the nunchaku slips outside, around and over your opponent's wrist. At the same time, step back with your left foot. (5) Grasp the weapon with your left hand also. (6-7) Then, with the handles over your opponent's grabbing wrist, apply a sharp downward pressure, bringing him down, and dislodge his hold.

DEFENSE AGAINST A LAPEL GRAB

(1) Hold the nunchaku, handles together, in your right hand and face your opponent. (2-4) As your opponent uses both his hands to grab your lapels, move into a two-handed grasp of your weapon, one handle held in each hand. Then, move the nunchaku up between your opponent's forearms. (5-8) Step back with your left foot. At the same time, slip the handles over and around his forearms, pulling him off balance. Apply a sharp downward pressure to dislodge his hands. (9-10) Swiftly shoot the tops of the handles into his eyes or throat. (11) Or, instead of striking with the handle tops, you may counter by using an upward snap of the handle bottoms into his throat or chin; (12-14) then, follow up with a downward strike into his eyes or face.

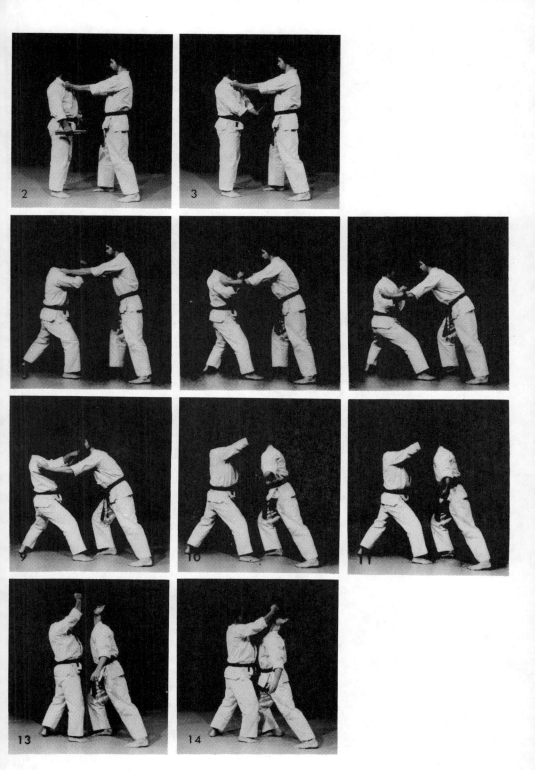

DEFENSE AGAINST
A NUNCHAKU GRAB,
TECHNIQUE I

(1) Hold the nunchaku, handles together, in your right hand and face your opponent. (2-3) As your opponent steps forward and grabs your weapon with his right hand, (4) reach up and close your left hand over the handle tops, thus positioning both your hands on either side of his. At the same time, step back with your left foot. (5-7) Begin rotating the nunchaku in a clockwise circle. Simultaneously, use the handles to pull upward, then push downward and out on your opponent's wrist. (8) As he comes down on his knee, pull the weapon back toward your right hip and (9) dislodge his hold. (10-11) Now, strike to the side of his face.

DEFENSE AGAINST
A NUNCHAKU GRAB, TECHNIQUE II

(1) Hold the nunchaku, handles together, in your right hand and face your opponent. (2-3) As your opponent steps forward and grabs your weapon with his left hand, (4-9) grasp his wrist with your left hand. At the same time, sweeping your left foot out, around and back, pivot counterclockwise 180 degrees on your right foot. As you turn, raise your opponent's left arm high overhead. (10-12) Then, drop your body and pull down sharply on his arm, throwing him off balance and to the ground on his back. (13-14) Pull your nunchaku free and, clasping both handles together in your right hand, raise it high to hit your opponent's face. (15-17) Or, instead of attacking him with both handles held together, release one of the handles and swing it down into his face.

112

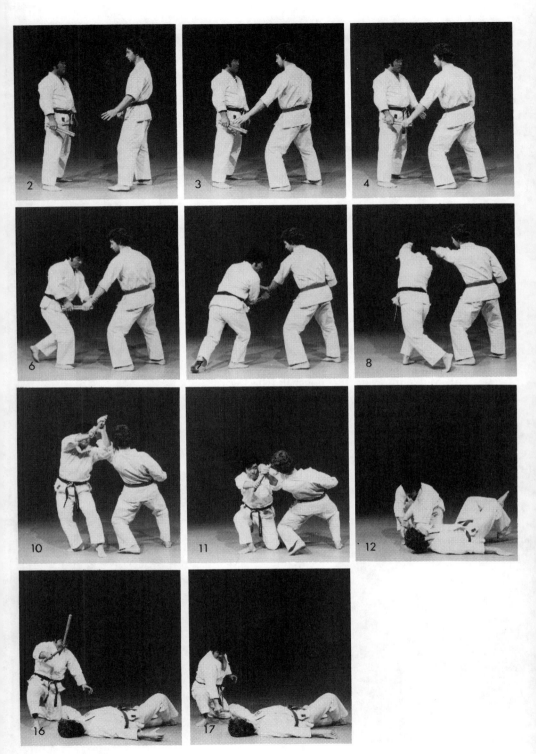

DEFENSE AGAINST A REAR GRAB
(1) As your opponent grabs you from behind, hold the nunchaku, handles together, in your right hand. (2-3) Raise the weapon and use the handle bottoms to strike his hands. (4-7) Step to the side with your left foot and swing the nunchaku backward and down into your opponent's groin. (8) Now, before he can recover, swiftly release one of the handles and (9-11) flip it upward, striking your opponent's face.

115

DEFENSE AGAINST
A PUNCH, TECHNIQUE I

(1) As your opponent prepares to attack with a right punch, hold the nunchaku, handles together, in your right hand. (2) Step to the outside with your left foot and (3-6) use the nunchaku to firmly deflect the blow to your low right. (7-9) Now, before your opponent can recover, swiftly and smoothly thrust the handle tops into his eyes.

117

DEFENSE AGAINST
A PUNCH, TECHNIQUE II

(1) As your opponent prepares to attack with a right punch, hold the nunchaku, handles together, in your right hand. (2-3) As he moves forward and the blow approaches, step back with your left foot and pivot counterclockwise into a gyaku-zenkutsu-dachi (rear defense stance). At the same time, swing the nunchaku inward to block the punch. (4-7) Then, before your opponent can recover and retract his extended right arm, swiftly use your left hand to grab hold of his right wrist. Simultaneously lower your body and forcefully shove the handle bottoms into his ribs. (8-9) In a smooth, fluid motion, drop beneath his right arm and bring the nunchaku over, around and under your opponent's right knee. (10-11) Come down on your left knee and, pulling on his right arm with your left hand, roll your opponent over your back and flip him to the ground. (12-14) Now, raise the nunchaku and strike downward to your opponent's face.

118

DEFENSE AGAINST A KNIFE ATTACK, TECHNIQUE I

(1) As your opponent prepares to attack with a knife, hold one handle in each of your hands. (2-3) As the knife thrust approaches, step back and out of range with your left foot. At the same time, bring the nunchaku over your opponent's attacking hand and pinch his wrist with the handles. (4-7) Keeping the nunchaku wrapped tightly around your opponent's wrist, pivot counterclockwise into a straddle stance. Simultaneously, pull his attacking arm and bring him forward and to the ground.

DEFENSE AGAINST A KNIFE ATTACK, TECHNIQUE II

(1) As your opponent prepares to attack with a knife, hold the nunchaku ready, handles together, in your right hand. (2) As the knife thrust approaches, release one of the handles and (3) swing it inward, knocking the blade from your opponent's hand. (4-6) Continue the swing, moving the nunchaku overhead in a clockwise circle. (7-9) As it comes forward again, strike across your opponent's face.

123

DEFENSE AGAINST A KICK

(1) As your opponent prepares to attack with a right front kick, hold the nunchaku, handles together, in your right hand. (2-3) As the kick approaches, step back and out of range with your left foot. At the same time, raise the nunchaku overhead with your right hand and deflect the blow with your left. (4-5) Continue to maintain control of your opponent's extended right leg and slam the handle bottoms into his shinbone. (6) Release his leg and pivot counterclockwise into a gyaku-zenkutsu-dachi (rear defense stance). (7-10) Free one of the nunchaku handles and, in a backhand swing, hit your opponent across the face and bring him down. Pivot clockwise into the blow as you strike.

DEFENSE AND COUNTER

(1) Grasping toward the bottom of each handle, use both hands to hold the nunchaku above you horizontally. (2) Release your left hand and, aiming the strike for your opponent's head, swing the weapon overhead in a clockwise circle. (3-4) As your opponent evades the blow, continue the sweep, (5) reaching back deeply to wrap the nunchaku around the back of your neck. Cross your left hand over your right and firmly grasp the free handle. (6) Release your right hand and, (7-9) using a backhand swing, hit across your opponent's face to bring him down.

DOUBLE NUNCHAKU DEFENSE AGAINST A KNIFE ATTACK

(1) As your opponent prepares to attack with a knife, clamp one handle of each weapon under an armpit. Firmly hold the other handle of each with your hands. (2-3) Push your right elbow outward and swiftly snap the nunchaku in your right hand forward and down to disarm your opponent. (4-6) Now, before he can recover, push your left el-

bow out and snap the nunchaku in your left hand forward and down to strike across your opponent's neck and face.

As is shown, using two nunchaku better equips a fighter to counter attacks. While it allows him twice the reach for offensive techniques, it also helps him stay safely out of his opponent's range.

kata

Unlike karate, kobu-do, particularly with respect to the nun-chaku, does not have any standardized kata or forms. Instead, the forms vary from one system to another, even from one master to another. The two fundamental and basic kata included in this section are taught by the authors to help develop overall proficiency with the nunchaku. Practicing them will help you to move skillfully and fluidly in all directions and against multiple attackers.

KATA I

(1) Assume a heisoku-dachi (ready stance). With your arms hanging naturally at your sides, hold the nunchaku, handles together, in your left hand. (2-3) Step to the side with your left foot. Simultaneously enter the kamae position. Bring both hands forward and hold the weapon, handles still together, before you. Then, grasp a handle in each hand and spread them before you. (4-8) Step forward with your right foot and come down on your left knee. At the same time, execute a right shoulder block, maneuvering the handle in your right hand up over your right shoulder, the handle in your left hand around your right arm to a position behind your right shoulder. (9-12) Release your left hand and swing the nunchaku in a "figure

10

eight." Then, in a continuous motion, sweep the loose handle to your left side, catching it firmly with your left hand. (13-14) Rise up out of the kneeling position. Step forward and to the side with your left foot to enter a kiba-dachi (horse stance). Hold the nunchaku before you horizontally. (15-16) Release your left hand. Strike to the rear over your right shoulder. (17-18) Then, swing the weapon forward and to your left at neck level. Reach back deeply with your right arm, allowing the nunchaku to wrap itself around the back of your neck. Cross your left arm beneath your right and grasp the

13

16

loose handle. (19) Release your right hand. (20-21) Bring the weapon up and around on your left side. (22-24) Then, execute a downward strike, allowing the nunchaku to hit against and recoil off your inner left thigh. (25-27) Strike upward. Cross your right hand under your left upper arm and catch the loose handle as it moves over and behind your left

28

shoulder. (28-29) Now, slip the nunchaku forward and around your left arm and shoulder. Uncross your arms and bring the weapon to a position before you, handles apart, your hands even, palms toward each other. (30-31) Execute a right shoulder block, maneuvering the handle in your right hand up over your right shoulder, the handle in your left hand around your right arm to a position behind your right shoulder. (32-33) Release your left hand and strike downward, allowing the nunchaku to hit against and bounce off your inner right thigh. (34-35) Reverse directions and swing the free handle upward. Use your open left hand to catch it firmly. (36) Shift your weight to your right foot.

31

34

29

30

32

33

35

36

(37-38) Then, step back with your left foot, shifting your weight to it, and assume a left kokutsu-dachi (back stance). At the same time, bring the nunchaku back around your right shoulder in a right shoulder block. (39-41) Slide your right foot back into a right kokutsu-dachi. Simultaneously slip the nunchaku forward and around your right arm and shoulder. Uncross your arms and bring the weapon to a position before you, handles spread, your hands even, palms facing the floor. (42) Step forward with your right foot and assume the yoi position.

37

40

KATA II

(1) Assume a heisoku-dachi (ready stance). With your arms hanging naturally at your sides, hold the nunchaku, handles together, in your left hand. (2-4) Assume the kamae position. Move your right foot into a heiko-dachi (natural stance). At the same time, grasping a handle in each hand, extend your arms and spread the weapon before you. (5-6) As you slide your right foot forward into a left kokutsu-dachi (back stance), execute a right shoulder block, maneuvering the handle in your right hand up over your right shoulder, the handle in your left hand around your right arm to a position behind your right shoulder. (7-9) Release your left hand. Swiftly snap the nunchaku over and down in a sharp overhead

10

strike. (10-12) On completing the movement, reverse directions and swing the weapon upward and back. Slip your left hand beneath your right arm. Catch the loose handle as it moves over and behind your right shoulder and return to the right shoulder block position. (13-16) As you slide your left foot forward into a right kokutsu-dachi, bring the nunchaku forward and around your right arm and shoulder to a position before you. Then, smoothly bring the weapon back and around your left arm and shoulder into a left shoulder block, maneuvering the handle in your left hand up over your left shoulder, the handle in your right around your left arm into a position behind your left shoulder. (17-21) Now, repeat the movements of nos. 7 to 12 with your left hand: Release your right hand and strike downward

13

16

144

19

on your left side. Then, reverse directions and swing the nunchaku upward and over your left shoulder,
slipping your right hand beneath
your left arm to catch the loose
handle. (22-24) Slide your right foot
forward and to the right. Simultaneously, pivot clockwise 90 degrees
into a left kokutsu-dachi. As you do
so, move the nunchaku forward and
around your left arm and shoulder to
a position before you. (25-26) Then,
smoothly bring the weapon back and
around your right arm and shoulder
into another right shoulder block.
(27-29) Now, release your left hand.
Whip the nunchaku out in a side

22

25

strike, swinging it horizontally to
your left, and allow it to hit against
and bounce off the left side of your
body. (30-31) Reverse directions
along the path of the side strike and
catch the loose handle with your left
hand. (32-35) As you pivot counterclockwise 180 degrees, slide your left
foot around and back. Shift your
weight to it and move your right foot
forward into a left kokutsu-dachi.
Simultaneously, maneuver the nunchaku forward and around your right
arm and shoulder into a right shoulder block. (36-40) Repeat the movements of nos. 27 to 31: Release your

37

left hand and whip the nunchaku to the left horizontally, allowing it to hit against and recoil off your left side. Then, reverse directions and catch the loose handle with your left hand. (41-43) As you pivot clockwise 90 degrees, bring your right foot out and around into a right zenkutsu-dachi (forward stance). Uncross the handles and hold them before you as you turn. (44) Shift your weight to your right leg and raise your left foot in preparation for a sharp mae-geri (front snap kick). (45) Deliver the

40

43

kick and (46) return your left foot to its retracted position. (47-49) Now, bring your left foot down behind you into a left kokutsu-dachi. At the same time, bring the nunchaku back and around your right arm and shoulder into a right shoulder block. (50-52) Release your left hand and horizontally sweep the nunchaku out to your left in a side strike. (53-54) Continuing the movement, swing the weapon overhead in a clockwise cir-

55

cle. (55-56) As it completes the rotation, reach back deeply with your right hand, allowing the nunchaku to wrap itself around the back of your neck. Cross your left hand over your right and grasp the free handle. (57-59) Release your right hand and swing the weapon in a clockwise circle on your left side. (60-62) As it comes down near your left leg, reverse directions and strike upward. Cross your right hand under your left upper arm, catching the loose handle as it moves over and behind your left shoulder, and execute a left shoulder block. (63-67) Move your right foot back and assume a right kokutsu-dachi. As you do so, move the nun-

58

61

64

chaku forward and around your left arm to a position before you. Then, smoothly bring it back and around your right arm and shoulder into a right shoulder block, maneuvering the handle in your right hand up over your right shoulder, the handle in your left around your right arm to a position behind your right shoulder. (68-69) Release your left hand and execute a diagonal side strike, allowing the nunchaku to hit against and recoil off the left side of your body. (70-73) Quickly reverse directions and swing the weapon over your

67

70

156

65

66

68

69

71

72

157

right shoulder and down behind you. Reach behind your back with your left hand, palm toward the ceiling, and catch the free handle. (74-77) Now, slide your left foot back and assume a left kokutsu-dachi. As you do so, raise your right arm overhead and slip the nunchaku forward and around your left shoulder. Extend the weapon before you, handles spread, your palms facing the floor. (78) Now, bring your left foot forward into a heiko-dachi and assume the yoi position.

73

76

74

75

77

78